~A BINGO BOOK~

# Massachusetts Bingo Book

## Complete Bingo Game in a Book

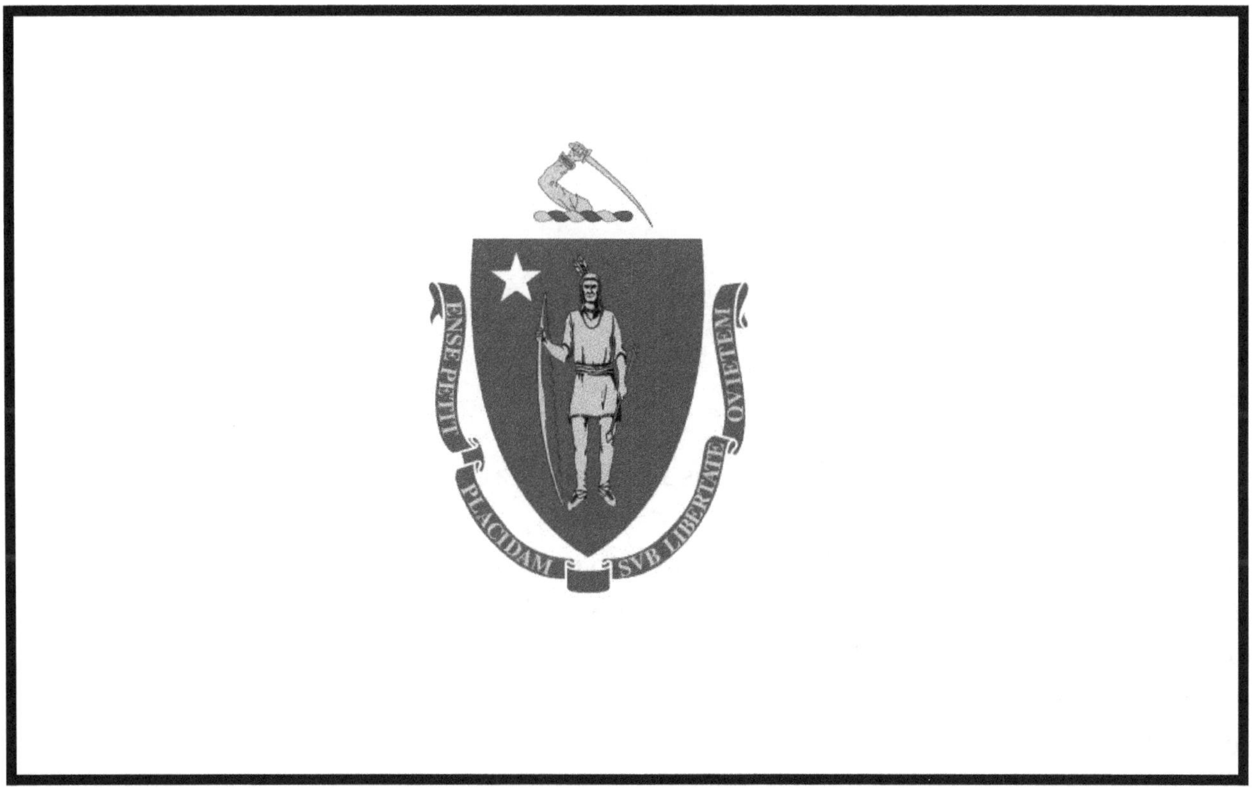


Written By Rebecca Stark

ISBN 978-0-87386-514-2

**Educational Books 'n' Bingo**

Printed in the U.S.A.

# DIRECTIONS

**INCLUDED:**

List of Terms

Templates for Additional Terms and Clues

2 Clues per Term

30 Unique Bingo Cards

Markers

1. **Either cut apart the book or make copies of ALL the sheets. You might want to make an extra copy of the clue sheets to use for introduction and review. Keep the sheets in an envelope for easy reuse.**
2. Cut apart the call cards with terms and clues.
3. Pass out one bingo card per student. There are enough for a class of 30.
4. Pass out markers. You may cut apart the markers included in this book or use any other small items of your choice.
5. Decide whether or not you will require the entire card to be filled. Requiring the entire card to be filled provides a better review. However, if you have a short time to fill, you may prefer to have them do the just the border or some other format. Tell the class before you begin what is required.
6. There are 50 terms. Read the list before you begin. If there are any terms that have not been covered in class, you may want to read to the students the term and clues before you begin.
7. There is a blank space in the middle of each card. You can instruct the students to use it as a free space or you can write in answers to cover terms not included. Of course, in this case you would create your own clues. (Templates provided.)
8. Shuffle the cards and place them in a pile. Two or three clues are provided for each term. If you plan to play the game with the same group more than once, you might want to choose a different clue for each game. If not, you may choose to use more than one clue.
9. Be sure to keep the cards you have used for the present game in a separate pile. When a student calls, "Bingo," he or she will have to verify that the correct answers are on his or her card AND that the markers were placed in response to the proper questions. Pull out the cards that are on the student's card keeping them in the order they were used in the game. Read each clue as it was given and ask the student to identify the correct answer from his or her card.
10. If the student has the correct answers on the card AND has shown that they were marked in response to the *correct questions,* then that student is the winner and the game is over. If the student does not have the correct answers on the card OR he or she marked the answers in response to *the wrong questions,* then the game continues until there is a proper winner.
11. If you want to play again, reshuffle the cards and begin again.

**Have fun!**

# TERMS INCLUDED

John Adams
John Quincy Adams
Samuel Adams
Susan B. Anthony
Berkshire(s)
Border(-ed)
Boston
Boston Massacre
Boston Tea Party
William Bradford
Bunker Hill
Cape Cod
John Chapman
Charles River
Coastal Lowland
Concord
Commonwealth
Connecticut Valley Lowland
Constitution
Calvin Coolidge
County (-ies)
Eastern New England Upland
Executive Branch
Flag
Benjamin Franklin
Theodor Geisel
Nathaniel Hawthorne
Industries
Judicial Branch
John F. Kennedy
King Phillip
Legislature
Lowell
Massachusetts Bay Colony
Mayflower
Motto
Mount Greylock
Patriots Day
Pilgrims
Plymouth Colony
Puritans
Paul Revere
Deborah Samson
Sons of Liberty
Springfield
Taconic Mountains
Thanksgiving
Western New England Upland
Witch Trials
Worcester

# Additional Terms

Choose as many additional terms as you would like and write them in the squares. Repeat each as desired.

Cut out the squares and randomly distribute them to the class.

Instruct the students to place their square on the center space of their card.

# Clues for Additional Terms

Write three clues for each of your additional terms.

| | |
|---|---|
| ______<br>1.<br>2.<br>3. | ______<br>1.<br>2.<br>3. |
| ______<br>1.<br>2.<br>3. | ______<br>1.<br>2.<br>3. |
| ______<br>1.<br>2.<br>3. | ______<br>1.<br>2.<br>3. |

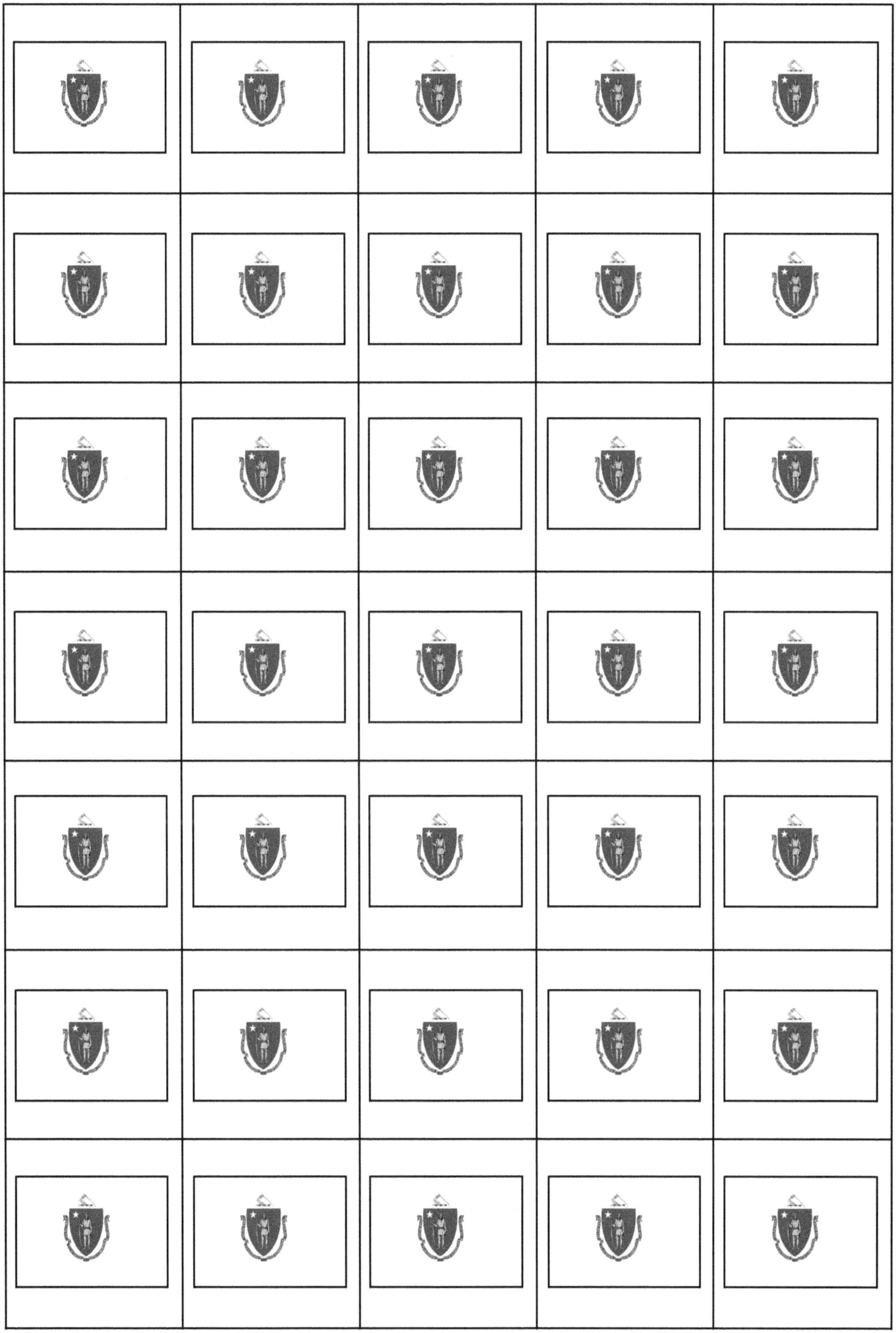

| | |
|---|---|
| **John Adams**<br>1. He was America's first vice-president and 2nd President.<br>2. ___ helped write a draft of the Declaration of Independence. | **John Quincy Adams**<br>1. This sixth President of the United States was born in Braintree, Massachusetts.<br>2. He was the son of the second President of the United States. |
| **Samuel Adams**<br>1. ___ was a leader of the Sons of Liberty. He organized the Boston Tea Party.<br>2. He is sometimes referred to as the "Father of the American Revolution." | **Susan B. Anthony**<br>1. This civil rights leader and suffragist was born in Adams, Massachusetts.<br>2. She dedicated her life to women's suffrage. |
| **Berkshire(s)**<br>1. The ___ Valley, which is less than 10 miles wide, runs between the ___ Hills to the east and the Taconic Mountains to the west.<br>2. Tanglewood, located in the ___, is the summer home of the Boston Symphony Orchestra. | **Border(-ed)**<br>1. New York, Vermont, New Hampshire, Connecticut, and Rhode Island ___ Massachusetts.<br>2. Massachusetts is ___ on the east by the Atlantic Ocean. |
| **Boston**<br>1. ___ is the capital of Massachusetts and the largest city in New England.<br>2. Faneuil Hall in ___ has served as a marketplace and a meeting hall since 1742. | **Boston Massacre**<br>1. The ___ refers to the killing of five colonists by British regulars on March 5, 1770. Another colonist died two weeks later.<br>2. Crispus Attucks, a sailor of African American and Native American descent, died as a result of the ___. |
| **Boston Tea Party**<br>1. The political protest known as the ___ was organized by the Sons of Liberty. It took place on December 16, 1773.<br>2. At the time, the ___ was usually called "the destruction of the tea." | **William Bradford**<br>1. ___ was the second governor of Plymouth Colony; he served for over 30 years.<br>2. Both he and John Carver were among the 41 signers of the *Mayflower Compact.* |

| | |
|---|---|
| **Bunker Hill**<br>1. The Battle of ___ took place on June 17, 1775, during the Siege of Boston.<br>2. The Battle of ___ was fought mainly on and around Breed's Hill. | **Cape Cod**<br>1. Provincetown is at the extreme tip of ___ in Barnstable County.<br>2. ___ is part of an archipelago consisting of a thin line of islands stretching toward New York, known as the Outer Lands. |
| **John Chapman**<br>1. Known as Johnny Appleseed, ___ is the official folk hero of Massachusetts. He was born in Leominster, Massachusetts, on September 26, 1774.<br>2. This pioneer became a folk hero by planting apple trees from New England to the Ohio River Valley. | **Charles River**<br>1. The ___ travels through 22 cities and towns. It flows from its source at Hopkinton to the Atlantic Ocean at Boston.<br>2. Harvard University, the oldest institution of higher learning in the United States, is located along the ___. |
| **Coastal Lowland**<br>1. The ___ region starts at the Atlantic Ocean and includes the Elizabeth Islands, Martha's Vineyard, and Nantucket Island.<br>2. The ___s are characterized by rounded hills, swamps, small lakes and ponds, and shallow streams and rivers.The region is east of the Eastern New England Upland region. | **Concord**<br>1. The battles of Lexington and ___ marked the start of the American Revolution.<br>2. Minute Man National Historical Park is located in ___. |
| **Commonwealth**<br>1. Massachusetts is one of four states to officially use the name ___. The others are Kentucky, Pennsylvania, and Virginia.<br>2. The original meaning of the word ___ was "a body governed by the people, not a king or tyrant." Today it has the same meaning as "state" when referring to Massachusetts. | **Connecticut Valley Lowland**<br>1. The___ is a long, narrow region that stretches from northern Massachusetts to southern Connecticut. It is west of the Eastern New England Upland.<br>2. The Connecticut River runs through this fertile region. In Massachusetts the ___ is about 20 miles wide. |
| **Constitution**<br>1. Massachusetts ratified the United States ___ on February 6, 1788, becoming the sixth state.<br>2. The Massachusetts ___ of 1780 is the oldest written ___ in continuous effect. It was the model for the ___ of the United States. | **Calvin Coolidge**<br>1. He was the 29th vice-president and the 30th President of the United States.<br>2. He was governor of Massachusetts before becoming vice-president. |

| | |
|---|---|
| **County (-ies)**<br>1. There are 14 ___ in Massachusetts.<br>2. Boston is in Suffolk ___. | **Eastern New England Upland**<br>1. The ___ region is bordered on the east by the Coastal Lowlands and the west by the Connecticut Valley Lowlands. It rises to about 1,000 feet above sea level.<br>2. The entire ___ region extends from Maine to New Jersey and is considered an extension of the White Mountains of New Hampshire. |
| **Executive Branch**<br>1. The governor is head of the ___. The present-day governor is [fill in].<br>2. The ___ of government enforces laws. It comprises the governor, lieutenant governor, attorney general, auditor, secretary of the commonwealth, and treasurer as well as the Governor's Council. | **Flag**<br>1. The coat of arms is on both sides of the state flag. It is centered on a field of white.<br>2. The coat of arms, which is on the state ___, depicts an Algonquin Native American with his arrow pointed downward as a sign of peace. |
| **Benjamin Franklin**<br>1. ___ is the official state inventor. He was born in Boston on January 17, 1706.<br>2. This founding father was a printer by trade. He was also an inventor, author, politician, postmaster, scientist, satirist, statesman, diplomat and more. | **Theodor Geisel**<br>1. Better known as Dr. Seuss, ___ is the official state children's author and illustrator. He wrote and illustrated 44 children's books. ___ was born in Springfield.<br>2. Although___ is the official children's author, Robert McCloskey's *Make Way for Ducklings* is the official state children's book. |
| **Nathaniel Hawthorne**<br>1. This novelist and short-story writer was born in Salem, Massachusetts.<br>2. His short stories were collected in a work entitled *Twice-Told Tales.* | **Industries**<br>1. Textiles, electronics, and publishing are major ___ of the state.<br>2. Education, tourism, and fishing are important ___ of the state. |
| **Judicial Branch**<br>1. The ___ interprets and applies the laws and ensures their constitutionality.<br>2. The Supreme Judicial Court is the highest court in the ___ of the Commonwealth. | **John F. Kennedy**<br>1. He was the 35th President of the United States; he was born in Brookline, Massachusetts.<br>2. When he was assassinated on November 22, 1963, Lyndon B. Johnson became President. His brother Robert was also assassinated. |

**King Phillip**
1. ___ was the son of Massasoit and chief of the Wampanoag nation; in his language, his name was Metacom or Metacomet.
2. ___'s War of 1675 to 1676 was a rebellion against Puritan incursions into Native American lands.

**Legislature**
1. The Massachusetts ___ is made up of the Senate and the House of Representatives.
2. The state ___ is known as the Great and General Court. There are 160 representatives and 40 senators in the Massachusetts ___.

**Lowell**
1. In 1840, the textile factories in ___ employed almost 8,000 workers; most were women between the ages of 16 and 35.
2. ___ National Historical Park preserves and interprets the history of the American Industrial Revolution there.

**Massachusetts Bay Colony**
1. The ___ included parts of what is now Massachusetts, Maine, New Hampshire, Rhode Island, and Connecticut.
2. Most settlers in the ___ were Puritans.

**Mayflower**
1. The Pilgrims came to the New World on the ___.
2. The "___ Compact" was signed by 41 of the settlers arriving at New Plymouth; it became the basis for government in the Plymouth Colony.

**Motto**
1. "By the sword we seek peace, but peace only under liberty" is the state ___.
2. The state ___ appears on the state flag; it is around the shield on a blue ribbon.

**Mount Greylock**
1. At 3,487 feet, ___ is the highest point in the state.
2. ___, the highest point in Massachusetts, is part of the Taconic Mountains, but it is often associated with the Berkshires.

**Patriots Day**
1. The third Monday in April is Patriots' Day in Massachusetts.
2. This holiday commemorates the anniversary of the battles of Lexington and Concord.

**Pilgrims**
1. The ___ broke with the Church of England and settled in Plymouth Colony.
2. Bradford and the other Plymouth settlers were not originally known as ___, but as "Old Comers."

**Plymouth Colony**
1. ___ was the first permanent settlement of Europeans in New England.
2. John Carver was the first governor of ___.

| | |
|---|---|
| **Puritans**<br>1. Led by John Winthrop, the ___ started Massachusetts Bay Colony.<br>2. The Pilgrims at Plymouth separated from the Anglican Church; the ___ at Massachusetts Bay did not. | **Paul Revere**<br>1. Along with William Dawes and others, ___ alerted the Minutemen that British forces were approaching before the battles of Lexington and Concord.<br>2. This Boston Patriot was a silversmith by trade. |
| **Deborah Samson**<br>1. ___ is the official state heroine. She impersonated a man so she could serve in the Continental Army.<br>2. ___ used the name Robert Shurtleff to enlist in the Continental Army. | **Sons of Liberty**<br>1. The ___ was started by Samuel Adams. It was formed to protect the rights of the colonists. Their motto became, "No taxation without representation."<br>2. The ___ organized and carried out the Boston Tea Party. |
| **Springfield**<br>1. ___ is the third most populous city in Massachusetts after Boston and Worcester.<br>2. ___ is sometimes called "The City of Firsts." Many innovations had their roots here, including the invention of basketball, the official state sport. | **Taconic Mountains**<br>1. The ___ are on the western border of Massachusetts, east of the Berkshire Valley.<br>2. The ___ are actually part of the Appalachian Mountains. |
| **Thanksgiving**<br>1. We celebrate ___ to remember the autumn harvest shared by the Plymouth colonists and Wampanoag Indians.<br>2. The autumn harvest feast shared by the Pilgrims and the Wampanoags was one of the first Thanksgiving celebrations in the colonies. | **Western New England Upland**<br>1. This land region is an extension of the Green Mountains of Vermont.<br>2. This land region is between the Connecticut Valley Lowlands and the Berkshire Valley. The Berkshire Hills are in this region. |
| **Witch Trials**<br>1. The Salem ___ were hearings and prosecutions of people accused of witch-craft in Colonial Massachusetts.<br>2. ___ took place from February 1692 to May 1693 in Salem and other parts of Colonial Massachusetts. | **Worcester**<br>1. ___ is the second largest city in New England.<br>2. This city is centrally located between Boston and Springfield. |

# Massachusetts Bingo

| | | | | |
|---|---|---|---|---|
| Plymouth Colony | John Adams | Samuel Adams | Constitution | Berkshire(s) |
| Commonwealth | John Quincy Adams | Witch Trials | King Phillip | Paul Revere |
| Western New England Upland | John F. Kennedy | | John Chapman | Worcester |
| Thanksgiving | Puritans | Taconic Mountains | Judicial Branch | Massachusetts Bay Colony |
| Motto | Executive Branch | Charles River | Sons of Liberty | Mount Greylock |

# Massachusetts Bingo

| | | | | |
|---|---|---|---|---|
| Thanksgiving | Western New England Upland | Nathaniel Hawthorne | Theodor Geisel | Industries |
| Massachusetts Bay Colony | Coastal Lowland | Boston Massacre | Puritans | Mayflower |
| William Bradford | Executive Branch | | Flag | Taconic Mountains |
| Patriots Day | Pilgrims | John F. Kennedy | Legislature | Berkshire(s) |
| Paul Revere | Witch Trials | Charles River | Commonwealth | Sons of Liberty |

# Massachusetts Bingo

| | | | | |
|---|---|---|---|---|
| Executive Branch | Taconic Mountains | Coastal Lowland | Judicial Branch | Western New England Upland |
| Massachusetts Bay Colony | John Quincy Adams | Boston Tea Party | John Adams | Eastern New England Upland |
| Puritans | Witch Trials | | Mayflower | Susan B. Anthony |
| John F. Kennedy | William Bradford | Motto | Patriots Day | Nathaniel Hawthorne |
| Sons of Liberty | Bunker Hill | Charles River | Legislature | Industries |

# Massachusetts Bingo

| | | | | |
|---|---|---|---|---|
| John F. Kennedy | Mayflower | Samuel Adams | Bunker Hill | Industries |
| Lowell | Boston | John Adams | Theodor Geisel | Western New England Upland |
| John Chapman | Patriots Day | | Mount Greylock | Constitution |
| Taconic Mountains | John Quincy Adams | Witch Trials | Charles River | Boston Massacre |
| Calvin Coolidge | Paul Revere | Border(-ed) | Sons of Liberty | Worcester |

# Massachusetts Bingo

| | | | | |
|---|---|---|---|---|
| Paul Revere | Berkshire(s) | Puritans | Boston Massacre | Bunker Hill |
| Lowell | Taconic Mountains | Boston Tea Party | Flag | John Quincy Adams |
| Samuel Adams | Worcester | | King Phillip | County (-ies) |
| Mount Greylock | Industries | Plymouth Colony | Legislature | Cape Cod |
| Coastal Lowland | Charles River | Western New England Upland | John F. Kennedy | John Chapman |

# Massachusetts Bingo

| | | | | |
|---|---|---|---|---|
| Susan B. Anthony | Mayflower | Nathaniel Hawthorne | Industries | Worcester |
| Judicial Branch | Puritans | Cape Cod | John Adams | Western New England Upland |
| Theodor Geisel | Calvin Coolidge | | Boston | Flag |
| Charles River | Motto | Legislature | Border(-ed) | Samuel Adams |
| Massachusetts Bay Colony | Boston Massacre | Plymouth Colony | John Chapman | Concord |

# Massachusetts Bingo

| | | | | |
|---|---|---|---|---|
| Plymouth Colony | Mayflower | County (-ies) | Taconic Mountains | Coastal Lowland |
| Massachusetts Bay Colony | Industries | Executive Branch | John Quincy Adams | Lowell |
| Worcester | Constitution | | Flag | Boston |
| John F. Kennedy | Patriots Day | Boston Tea Party | Thanksgiving | William Bradford |
| Charles River | Bunker Hill | Legislature | Border(-ed) | Susan B. Anthony |

# Massachusetts Bingo

| | | | | |
|---|---|---|---|---|
| John Chapman | Mayflower | Connecticut Valley Lowland | Judicial Branch | Boston |
| Lowell | Samuel Adams | Theodor Geisel | Worcester | Boston Massacre |
| Concord | Bunker Hill | | Industries | Berkshire(s) |
| Sons of Liberty | John F. Kennedy | Thanksgiving | Calvin Coolidge | Patriots Day |
| Witch Trials | Charles River | Border(-ed) | Puritans | Massachusetts Bay Colony |

# Massachusetts Bingo

| | | | | |
|---|---|---|---|---|
| Flag | Coastal Lowland | Executive Branch | Concord | Bunker Hill |
| Calvin Coolidge | Industries | John Chapman | Puritans | Mayflower |
| Eastern New England Upland | Plymouth Colony | | John Quincy Adams | Connecticut Valley Lowland |
| Cape Cod | Berkshire(s) | Motto | King Phillip | County (-ies) |
| Patriots Day | Legislature | Boston Tea Party | Thanksgiving | Mount Greylock |

# Massachusetts Bingo

| | | | | |
|---|---|---|---|---|
| Thanksgiving | Judicial Branch | Boston | Theodor Geisel | Concord |
| Worcester | Boston Massacre | John Adams | John Quincy Adams | Industries |
| Bunker Hill | Mayflower | | Constitution | William Bradford |
| Motto | Mount Greylock | Cape Cod | Legislature | Eastern New England Upland |
| Boston Tea Party | Massachusetts Bay Colony | Nathaniel Hawthorne | Paul Revere | John Chapman |

# Massachusetts Bingo

| | | | | |
|---|---|---|---|---|
| Susan B. Anthony | Mayflower | Puritans | Cape Cod | Massachusetts Bay Colony |
| Connecticut Valley Lowland | Eastern New England Upland | King Phillip | Flag | John Adams |
| Lowell | Industries | | Nathaniel Hawthorne | Executive Branch |
| Boston Tea Party | Western New England Upland | Legislature | Bunker Hill | Thanksgiving |
| Calvin Coolidge | Charles River | Plymouth Colony | Border(-ed) | Coastal Lowland |

# Massachusetts Bingo

| | | | | |
|---|---|---|---|---|
| Coastal Lowland | Berkshire(s) | Eastern New England Upland | Judicial Branch | Flag |
| Executive Branch | Massachusetts Bay Colony | Samuel Adams | Border(-ed) | John Quincy Adams |
| Plymouth Colony | County (-ies) | | Worcester | Theodor Geisel |
| Charles River | Patriots Day | Industries | Thanksgiving | Lowell |
| Mayflower | Connecticut Valley Lowland | Bunker Hill | Calvin Coolidge | Boston Massacre |

# Massachusetts Bingo

| | | | | |
|---|---|---|---|---|
| Cape Cod | Berkshire(s) | Susan B. Anthony | Eastern New England Upland | Worcester |
| Samuel Adams | Connecticut Valley Lowland | Industries | Flag | William Bradford |
| Judicial Branch | Boston Massacre | | Executive Branch | County (-ies) |
| John Chapman | Legislature | Boston | Bunker Hill | Thanksgiving |
| Charles River | Mount Greylock | Border(-ed) | Plymouth Colony | King Phillip |

# Massachusetts Bingo

| | | | | |
|---|---|---|---|---|
| Commonwealth | Industries | Puritans | Flag | Calvin Coolidge |
| Boston Massacre | Plymouth Colony | Eastern New England Upland | John Quincy Adams | Mayflower |
| Cape Cod | Constitution | | Nathaniel Hawthorne | Boston Tea Party |
| Mount Greylock | Legislature | Bunker Hill | Boston | Susan B. Anthony |
| Charles River | Theodor Geisel | William Bradford | Massachusetts Bay Colony | John Chapman |

# Massachusetts Bingo

| | | | | |
|---|---|---|---|---|
| King Phillip | Flag | Puritans | Coastal Lowland | Judicial Branch |
| Susan B. Anthony | Nathaniel Hawthorne | John Adams | Samuel Adams | Calvin Coolidge |
| Worcester | Plymouth Colony | | Western New England Upland | Mayflower |
| Charles River | Eastern New England Upland | Connecticut Valley Lowland | Legislature | Cape Cod |
| Massachusetts Bay Colony | Patriots Day | Border(-ed) | Concord | Executive Branch |

# Massachusetts Bingo

| | | | | |
|---|---|---|---|---|
| Boston | Eastern New England Upland | Connecticut Valley Lowland | Concord | Pilgrims |
| Theodor Geisel | William Bradford | County (-ies) | Lowell | Constitution |
| Cape Cod | Berkshire(s) | | Worcester | Executive Branch |
| John F. Kennedy | Boston Massacre | Charles River | King Phillip | Thanksgiving |
| Calvin Coolidge | Springfield | Border(-ed) | Patriots Day | Mayflower |

# Massachusetts Bingo

| | | | | |
|---|---|---|---|---|
| Boston Tea Party | Deborah Samson | Benjamin Franklin | Eastern New England Upland | Commonwealth |
| King Phillip | Calvin Coolidge | Legislature | Constitution | County (-ies) |
| Flag | John Chapman | | Springfield | Connecticut Valley Lowland |
| Mount Greylock | Massachusetts Bay Colony | Thanksgiving | Puritans | William Bradford |
| Motto | Cape Cod | Coastal Lowland | Judicial Branch | Berkshire(s) |

# Massachusetts Bingo

| | | | | |
|---|---|---|---|---|
| Concord | Bunker Hill | Boston Massacre | Cape Cod | Theodor Geisel |
| Mayflower | Boston Tea Party | Motto | Worcester | Calvin Coolidge |
| Flag | William Bradford | | Benjamin Franklin | Samuel Adams |
| Berkshire(s) | John Adams | Legislature | Thanksgiving | Nathaniel Hawthorne |
| Springfield | Eastern New England Upland | Puritans | Deborah Samson | Susan B. Anthony |

# Massachusetts Bingo

| | | | | |
|---|---|---|---|---|
| Worcester | Susan B. Anthony | Eastern New England Upland | Connecticut Valley Lowland | Thanksgiving |
| King Phillip | Judicial Branch | Mayflower | Coastal Lowland | Constitution |
| Deborah Samson | Bunker Hill | | John Quincy Adams | Western New England Upland |
| Nathaniel Hawthorne | Springfield | Motto | Patriots Day | Benjamin Franklin |
| Samuel Adams | Pilgrims | Massachusetts Bay Colony | John Chapman | Border(-ed) |

# Massachusetts Bingo

| | | | | |
|---|---|---|---|---|
| Commonwealth | Deborah Samson | Judicial Branch | Eastern New England Upland | Border(-ed) |
| Boston Massacre | Executive Branch | Lowell | Motto | Theodor Geisel |
| Berkshire(s) | County (-ies) | | John F. Kennedy | John Adams |
| Paul Revere | Witch Trials | Sons of Liberty | Patriots Day | Springfield |
| Taconic Mountains | John Chapman | Pilgrims | Thanksgiving | Benjamin Franklin |

# Massachusetts Bingo

| | | | | |
|---|---|---|---|---|
| King Phillip | Susan B. Anthony | Lowell | Eastern New England Upland | Paul Revere |
| Berkshire(s) | Benjamin Franklin | Boston | Connecticut Valley Lowland | Plymouth Colony |
| William Bradford | Massachusetts Bay Colony | | Deborah Samson | Puritans |
| Motto | Coastal Lowland | Springfield | Mount Greylock | John Chapman |
| John F. Kennedy | Pilgrims | Border(-ed) | Boston Tea Party | Patriots Day |

# Massachusetts Bingo

| | | | | |
|---|---|---|---|---|
| Concord | Nathaniel Hawthorne | Benjamin Franklin | Samuel Adams | Cape Cod |
| Theodor Geisel | Judicial Branch | Western New England Upland | Connecticut Valley Lowland | John Quincy Adams |
| Boston Massacre | Constitution | | Plymouth Colony | County (-ies) |
| Springfield | Mount Greylock | Patriots Day | John Adams | Lowell |
| Pilgrims | Boston Tea Party | Deborah Samson | William Bradford | John F. Kennedy |

# Massachusetts Bingo

| | | | | |
|---|---|---|---|---|
| Boston | Deborah Samson | Coastal Lowland | Samuel Adams | Border(-ed) |
| Susan B. Anthony | Commonwealth | Massachusetts Bay Colony | King Phillip | John Adams |
| Nathaniel Hawthorne | Cape Cod | | Sons of Liberty | Plymouth Colony |
| William Bradford | Pilgrims | Springfield | Boston Tea Party | Patriots Day |
| Paul Revere | Witch Trials | John Chapman | Motto | Benjamin Franklin |

# Massachusetts Bingo

| | | | | |
|---|---|---|---|---|
| Boston | John Chapman | Commonwealth | Deborah Samson | Connecticut Valley Lowland |
| Benjamin Franklin | Border(-ed) | Lowell | Theodor Geisel | Plymouth Colony |
| County (-ies) | Concord | | Cape Cod | William Bradford |
| Paul Revere | Sons of Liberty | Springfield | Boston Tea Party | Berkshire(s) |
| Taconic Mountains | John F. Kennedy | Pilgrims | Judicial Branch | Witch Trials |

# Massachusetts Bingo

| | | | | |
|---|---|---|---|---|
| John F. Kennedy | Lowell | Deborah Samson | Puritans | Benjamin Franklin |
| John Adams | Berkshire(s) | King Phillip | Boston | John Quincy Adams |
| Mount Greylock | Connecticut Valley Lowland | | Sons of Liberty | Springfield |
| Western New England Upland | Paul Revere | Witch Trials | Pilgrims | Constitution |
| Border(-ed) | Commonwealth | Boston Massacre | Calvin Coolidge | Taconic Mountains |

# Massachusetts Bingo

| | | | | |
|---|---|---|---|---|
| Benjamin Franklin | Deborah Samson | Nathaniel Hawthorne | Theodor Geisel | Concord |
| Motto | Judicial Branch | Connecticut Valley Lowland | Commonwealth | Boston |
| Mount Greylock | Sons of Liberty | | Constitution | John F. Kennedy |
| Boston Tea Party | Samuel Adams | Paul Revere | Pilgrims | Springfield |
| County (-ies) | Calvin Coolidge | Puritans | Witch Trials | Taconic Mountains |

# Massachusetts Bingo

| | | | | |
|---|---|---|---|---|
| Nathaniel Hawthorne | Boston Massacre | Deborah Samson | Commonwealth | Executive Branch |
| Paul Revere | Sons of Liberty | King Phillip | Springfield | John Quincy Adams |
| Legislature | Witch Trials | | Pilgrims | John F. Kennedy |
| Concord | Susan B. Anthony | Lowell | Taconic Mountains | John Adams |
| Calvin Coolidge | Constitution | Benjamin Franklin | Western New England Upland | County (-ies) |

# Massachusetts Bingo

| | | | | |
|---|---|---|---|---|
| Nathaniel Hawthorne | Commonwealth | Western New England Upland | Deborah Samson | Boston |
| Executive Branch | Benjamin Franklin | Sons of Liberty | Theodor Geisel | Constitution |
| Witch Trials | William Bradford | | County (-ies) | Motto |
| Thanksgiving | Concord | Massachusetts Bay Colony | Pilgrims | Springfield |
| Samuel Adams | Flag | Calvin Coolidge | Taconic Mountains | Paul Revere |

# Massachusetts Bingo

| | | | | |
|---|---|---|---|---|
| Benjamin Franklin | Commonwealth | Concord | King Phillip | Flag |
| Patriots Day | Motto | Lowell | County (-ies) | Western New England Upland |
| Mount Greylock | Sons of Liberty | | John Quincy Adams | Deborah Samson |
| Executive Branch | Paul Revere | Industries | Pilgrims | Springfield |
| Boston | Connecticut Valley Lowland | Taconic Mountains | Susan B. Anthony | Witch Trials |

# Massachusetts Bingo

| | | | | |
|---|---|---|---|---|
| Bunker Hill | Deborah Samson | Theodor Geisel | Flag | Springfield |
| John Adams | Commonwealth | Nathaniel Hawthorne | Constitution | John Quincy Adams |
| Mount Greylock | Cape Cod | | County (-ies) | Lowell |
| Taconic Mountains | Susan B. Anthony | Samuel Adams | Pilgrims | Sons of Liberty |
| Paul Revere | Worcester | Witch Trials | Benjamin Franklin | Western New England Upland |

www.ingramcontent.com/pod-product-compliance
Lightning Source LLC
LaVergne TN
LVHW061338060426
835511LV00014B/1986